TV COOKS

Ken Hom

Noodles and Rice

BBC

Published by BBC Worldwide Limited,
Woodlands, 80 Wood Lane,
London W12 0TT

The recipes in this book first appeared in the following:
Ken Hom's Quick & Easy Chinese Cookery
© Taurom Incorporated 1989
Ken Hom's Vegetarian Cookery
© Taurom Incorporated 1987 and 1995

This edition first published 1998
© Promo Group Limited 1998
The moral right of the author has been asserted

ISBN 0 563 38454 9

Photographs: Juliet Piddington
© BBC Worldwide Limited 1998

Project Editor: Charlotte Lochhead
Copy Editor: Pam Mallender
Design: Town Group Creative
Stylist and Home Economist:
Sarah Ramsbottom
Author photograph: Chris King

Set in New Caledonia and Helvetica
Printed and bound in France by
Imprimerie Pollina S.A., Luçon, France
Colour separations by
Imprimerie Pollina S.A.
Cover printed by Imprimerie Pollina S.A.

Cover and frontispiece:
Stir-fried Vegetables over a Rice Noodle Cloud

CONTENTS

RECIPE NOTES

Wash all fresh produce before preparation and peel as necessary.

Spoon measurements are level. Always use proper measuring spoons:
1 teaspoon = 5ml and 1 tablespoon = 15ml.

Never mix metric or imperial measures in one recipe. Stick to one or the other.

Nutritional notes are for a single portion, serving one person, when the dish is made for the number of servings stated in the recipe (unless indicated otherwise). The nutritional analysis of deep-fried recipes are provided on the basis of an estimated amount of oil absorbed in cooking.

Anyone with an allergy to nuts should substitute groundnut oil for corn oil.

Eggs are medium. If your kitchen is warm, keep the eggs in the fridge, but allow them to come to room temperature before using. While the proven risks of healthy people becoming ill from eating fresh raw eggs are minimal, pregnant women, the sick, the elderly and the very young should avoid eating raw or partially cooked eggs.

HANDY CONVERSION TABLES

Weight		Volume		Linear	
15g	½oz	30ml	1fl oz	5mm	¼in
25g	1oz	50ml	2fl oz	10mm/1cm	½in
40g	1½oz	100ml	3½fl oz	2cm	¾in
55g	2oz	125ml	4fl oz	2.5cm	1in
85g	3oz	150ml	5fl oz (¼ pint)	5cm	2in
115g	4oz	175ml	6fl oz	7.5cm	3in
140g	5oz	200ml	7fl oz (⅓ pint)	10cm	4in
175g	6oz	225ml	8fl oz	13cm	5in
200g	7oz	250ml	9fl oz	15cm	6in
225g	8oz	300ml	10fl oz (½ pint)	18cm	7in
250g	9oz	350ml	12fl oz	20cm	8in
280g	10oz	400ml	14fl oz	23cm	9in
350g	12oz	425ml	15fl oz (¾ pint)	25cm	10in
375g	13oz	450ml	16fl oz	28cm	11in
400g	14oz	500ml	18fl oz	30cm	12in
425g	15oz	600ml	20fl oz (1 pint)		
450g	1lb	700ml	1¼ pints		
550g	1¼lb	850ml	1½ pints		
750g	1lb 10oz	1 litre	1¾ pints		
900g	2lb	1.2 litres	2 pints		
1kg	2¼lb	1.3 litres	2¼ pints		
1.3kg	3lb	1.4 litres	2½ pints		
1.8kg	4lb	1.7 litres	3 pints		
2.25kg	5lb	2 litres	3½ pints		
		2.5 litres	4½ pints		

Ⓥ **Suitable for vegetarians**

All authentic Chinese meals include two main food types. One is the *cai*, which consists of meat, poultry, fish and vegetable dishes. The other is the *fan* and includes anything made from wheat or rice – from wonton skins and rice paper to noodles and rice itself. It is because these foods are such staples in Chinese cuisine, that they merit a book in themselves.

Contrary to popular depictions, many Chinese rely heavily on grains like wheat, instead of rice, because in the drier, colder northern areas of the country rice cannot be cultivated. Wheat and rice, and the flours they produce, have given rise to a wide variety of noodles and, in turn, this allows for endless combinations of flavours and textures to be brought together to create a fabulous array of appetising dishes. Many of the recipes chosen here are quick and easy, perfect for today's fast pace of life, and most have tips to ensure success in the kitchen. Some of the recipes come from countries other than China, and you will also find 'fusion' dishes blending the best of the flavours from east and west.

Noodles and rice are not only integral to Chinese cookery they are also, in China, the very fundamentals of life. As one Chinese sage put it: 'Without meats the food is less tasteful, but without the noodle or rice one's hunger cannot be satisfied'. As you can imagine, I'm a great fan of noodles and rice and I hope that, once you have cooked some of the recipes in this book, you will be too.

Ken Hom

INGREDIENTS

Chinese dried mushrooms

There are many varieties of these wonderful mushrooms, said to have been produced for more than 1000 years in southern China. Black or brown, they add a particular flavour and aroma to Chinese dishes. The very large ones, with a lighter colour and a highly cracked surface, are the best and so are usually the more expensive. They can be bought in boxes or plastic bags from Chinese grocers and are fairly pricey, but a little does go a long way. Keep stored in an airtight jar in a cool, dry place.

Chinese dried cloud ears (black fungus): these tiny mushrooms are known as cloud ears because when soaked, they look like little clouds. They are valued for their crunchy texture and slightly smokey flavour.

Chinese dried wood ears: these are a larger variety of cloud ears. Once soaked, they will swell up to four or five times their size. Cut away any hard pieces.

Groundnut (peanut) oil

This is also known as peanut oil or arachide oil. I prefer to use groundnut oil, because it has a pleasant, mild taste which is unobtrusive. Although it has a higher saturated fat content than some oil, its ability to be heated to a high temperature without burning makes it perfect for stir frying and deep-frying. Many supermarkets do stock groundnut oil but if you can't find it, or have an allergy to nuts, use corn oil.

Noodles

Pasta or noodles come in many forms in China, Japan and Southeast Asia and have been part of the diet of this region for many hundreds of years. If you cannot find the type you need in your supermarket, they will be available in a Chinese grocers.

Wheat noodles and egg noodles: made from hard or soft wheat flour and water, these are available fresh and dried. If egg has been added, they are usually labelled as egg noodles or sometimes Chinese egg noodles. Flat noodles are often used in soups, while rounded noodles can be better for stir frying, but there are no hard-and-fast rules and there are a variety of shapes and sizes to chose. Well wrapped fresh noodles can be frozen successfully. Defrost thoroughly before using. If you are cooking noodles in advance before using in another dish or for stir frying, toss the cooked drained noodles in one to two teaspoons of sesame oil. Cover with plastic film and keep in the fridge for up to two hours.

Rice noodles: these are very popular in southern China and throughout Southeast Asia. They are white, come in a variety of shapes and names – from wide flat ones to vermicelli-thin round ones, and those called 'fun' noodles – and are usually dried. One of the most common is rice stick noodles, which are flat and about the length of a chopstick. They can also vary in thickness. Try to use the type called for in the recipe to give the best results.

Bean thread (transparent) noodles: these are also called cellophane noodles. They are made from ground mung beans and not from a grain flour. They are available dried, are very fine and white and easily recognised packed in their neat, plastic-wrapped bundles. They are never served on their own, but are added to soups or braised dishes or are deep-fried as a garnish. If you do need to separate them in their dried form, place in a large paper bag and pull them apart. Do not soak them before frying.

Rice

For all the recipes in this book, fill a glass measuring jug with rice to the 425ml/15fl oz level. Although the Chinese still go through the ritual of washing rice, I believe this step can be bypassed with rice bought at supermarkets.

Long grain: this is the most popular rice for Asian food and is my own favourite. It is worth trying to find the Thai aromatic long grain rice, now available. It has a pleasing fragrance similar to the basmati rice used in Indian cuisine.

Short grain: this is not to be confused with pudding rice. Varieties known as American Rose or Japanese Rose are suitable and can be found in Chinese grocers. Short grain is slightly stickier than long grain rice, but it is cooked in the same way.

Glutinous rice: this is also known as sweet or sticky rice. It is short, round and pearl-like and is not be be confused with ordinary short grain or pudding rice. It is sweeter and stickier than ordinary rice when cooked. Most Chinese grocers stock it, and it must be soaked for at least two hours, preferably overnight, before cooking. You may cook it in the same way as long grain rice or by steaming.

Rice papers

Vietnamese rice papers are often beautifully textured by the imprint of the bamboo trays on which they are placed to dry. They are very thin dried sheets, usually round, and are used as wrappers for Vietnamese-style spring rolls. Unlike Chinese wrappers, the filled rice papers can be stored in the fridge for up to three hours before frying. Once fried, they can be kept crisp in a low oven for up to two hours.

Rice wine/Chinese rice wine

An important flavour of Chinese cuisine, it is used extentisively throughout China for cooking and drinking. There are many varieties, the finest believed to be that from Shaoxing in Zhijiang Province in eastern China. It is made from glutinous rice, yeast and spring water. Store it, tightly corked, at room temperature. Good-quality, pale dry sherry can be substituted but cannot equal rice wine's rich, mellow taste.

Sichuan peppercorns

These are known in China as 'flower peppers' because they look like flower buds opening. They are reddish brown with a strong pungent odour, which distinguishes them from the hotter black peppercorns. Sichuan peppercorns are not from peppers at all, but are the dried berries of a shrub which is a member of the citrus family. I find their smell reminds me of lavender, while their taste is sharp and mildly spicy.

Sichuan preserved vegetable

A speciality of Sichuan Province, this is the root of the mustard green which is pickled in salt and hot chillies. Sold in tins in Chinese grocers, it gives a pleasantly crunchy texture and spicy taste to dishes. Before using, rinse in cold water, then slice or chop as required. Any unused vegetable can be transferred to a jar with a tight-fitting lid and stored in the fridge where it can be kept indefinitely.

Sugar

Properly employed, sugar helps balance the various flavours of sauces and other dishes. Chinese sugar comes in several forms: rock or yellow lump sugar, brown sugar slabs and as maltose or malt sugar. I particularly like to use rock sugar, which is rich and has a more subtle flavour than refined granulated sugar. It also gives a good lustre or glaze to braised dishes and sauces. You can buy this in Chinese grocers. You may need to break the lumps into smaller pieces with a wooden mallet or rolling pin. If you cannot find it, use white sugar or coffee sugar crystals (the amber chunky kind) instead.

Wonton skins

These, like noodles, are made from egg and flour and can be bought fresh or frozen from Chinese grocers. They are thin pastry-like wrappings which can be stuffed with sweet or savoury fillings, and fried, steamed or used in soups. They are sold in little piles of 8cm/3¼in yellowish squares, wrapped in plastic. The number of squares or skins varies between 30-36 depending on the supplier. Fresh skins will keep for up to five days if stored in plastic film or a plastic bag in the fridge. If you are using frozen skins, just peel off the number you need and defrost thoroughly before using.

1. Bamboo shoots
2. Sichuan preserved vegetables
3. Yellow bean sauce
4. Curry paste
5. Sesame oil
6. Chilli bean sauce
7. Peanuts skinned and with skins
8. Wonton skins
9. Rice papers
10. Fresh root ginger
11. Chinese rock sugar
12. Dried wood ear mushrooms
13. Dried cloud ear mushrooms
14. Dried shiitake mushrooms
15. Black beans
16. Chinese cinnamon bark
17. Sesame seeds
18. Sichuan peppercorns
19. Asparagus
20. Chillies
21. Coriander
22. Fresh peas
23. Chinese long beans
24. Bean sprouts
25. Mangetout
26. Soft beancurd
27. Glutinous rice
28. Long grain rice
29. Dried Chinese 'fun' rice noodles
30. Bean thread (transparent) noodles
31. Fresh noodles
32. Dried noodles

Soups

SOFT BEANCURD AND SPINACH SOUP ⓥ

Serves 4

55g/2oz bean thread (transparent) noodles

1.2 litres/2 pints Vegetable stock (page 62)

750g/1lb 10oz fresh spinach, stalks removed and washed

2 tbsp light soy sauce

3 tbsp Chinese rice wine or dry sherry

2 tsp sugar

½ tsp salt

225g/8oz soft beancurd, cut into 2.5cm/1in cubes

1   Soak the noodles in a large bowl of warm water for 15 minutes. When soft, drain and discard the water. Using scissors or a knife, cut the noodles into 7.5cm/3in lengths.

2   Place the stock in a pan and bring to simmering point. Add the noodles and simmer for 2 minutes. Add all the remaining ingredients, except the beancurd and simmer for 2 minutes. Gently add the beancurd and simmer for 2 minutes or until heated through.

Nutrition notes per serving: *174 Calories, Protein 12g, Carbohydrate 18g, Fat 5g, Saturated fat 1g, Fibre 4g, Added sugar 3g, Salt 3.37g.*

TIP

Use soft beancurd for this soup – its custard-like texture and mild flavour work with the sugar to neutralise the metallic edge of the spinach.

INDONESIAN CAULIFLOWER SOUP ⓥ

Serves 2–4

1 tbsp groundnut (peanut) oil

1 tbsp finely chopped garlic

1 small onion, finely chopped

1½ tsp salt

¼ tsp freshly ground black pepper

1 tsp ground coriander

2 tsp ground cumin

1.2 litres/2 pints Vegetable stock (page 62)

450g/1lb cauliflower, cut into 2.5–4cm/1–1½in wide florets

115g/4oz dried or fresh egg noodles

fresh coriander leaves, to garnish

1   Heat a wok or large frying pan and add the oil. Add the garlic, onion, half a teaspoon of the salt, the pepper, ground coriander and cumin and stir fry for 2 minutes. Add the stock and cauliflower florets and simmer for 20 minutes or until the cauliflower is tender.

2   Stir in the noodles and cook for 8–10 minutes if using dried noodles, or 4–5 minutes for fresh noodles.

3   Add the remaining salt and give the soup a good stir. Serve garnished with the fresh coriander leaves.

Nutrition notes per serving when dish serves 2: *401 Calories, Protein 18g, Carbohydrate 56g, Fat 14g, Saturated fat 1g, Fibre 5g, Added sugar 0g, Salt 6g.*

SIZZLING RICE SOUP Ⓥ

25g/1oz Chinese dried mushrooms

15g/½oz Chinese dried wood ears or large cloud ears

1.2 litres/2 pints Vegetable stock (page 62)

4 tbsp finely chopped spring onions

3 tbsp Chinese rice wine or dry sherry

2 tbsp light soy sauce

450g/1lb soft beancurd, cut into 1cm/½in cubes

2 tsp Chilli oil (See Tip, page 19), optional

½ tsp salt

600ml/1 pint groundnut (peanut) oil, for deep-frying

1 rice cake (recipe follows)

fresh coriander leaves, to garnish

1 In separate bowls, soak the dried mushrooms and wood ears in warm water for 20 minutes. Drain and squeeze out any excess liquid. Trim off the tough stalks and discard, then shred the mushroom caps and wood ears into 5cm/2in strips.

2 Bring the stock to simmering point in a large pan. Add the mushrooms, spring onions, rice wine or sherry, soy sauce, beancurd, Chilli oil, if desired, and salt. Simmer for 20 minutes before transferring to a serving bowl.

3 Meanwhile, heat the oil in a large frying pan or wok until it is nearly smoking. Drop in a grain of rice to test the heat – the rice should bubble all over and immediately come to the surface.

4 Break up the rice cake and deep-fry the pieces for 1–2 minutes until they puff up and brown slightly. Using a slotted spoon, remove immediately and drain on kitchen paper. Quickly transfer to a plate, then slide into the soup. It should sizzle dramatically. Garnish with fresh coriander.

Nutrition notes per serving, excluding rice cake: *148 Calories, Protein 10g, Carbohydrate 9g, Fat 7g, Saturated fat 1g, Fibre trace, Added sugar trace, Salt 2.71g.*

RICE CAKE Ⓥ

225ml/8fl oz long grain white rice, washed

2 tsp groundnut (peanut) oil

1 Tip the rice into a 23cm/9in wide, heavy pan with 600ml/1 pint of water. Bring the water to the boil over a high heat. Reduce the heat to as low as possible, cover and cook the rice for 45 minutes. The rice should form a heavy crust on the base of the pan. Remove all the loose surface rice, leaving the thick crust. Use the loose rice for making any of the fried rice dishes in this book.

2 Dribble the oil evenly over the top of the rice cake left in the pan, and cook over a very low heat for 5 minutes. The cake should lift off evenly at this point. If it is still sticky, add another teaspoon of oil and cook until the whole cake comes loose. Transfer to a plate to dry out until needed.

Nutrition notes per rice cake: *866 Calories, Protein 15g, Carbohydrate 195g, Fat 8g, Saturated fat 1g, Fibre 0g, Added sugar 0g, Salt 0.03g.*

TIP

Once cooked, the rice cake can be left at room temperature for several days. Let the rice cake dry out: do not cover it, as moisture will form and make it soggy. Cut it into pieces and deep-fry just before serving your soup. Very hot oil ensures that the pieces become crispy and not greasy – almost like dried popcorn.

FRAGRANT NOODLE SOUP Ⓥ

Serves 2–4

225g/8oz dried or fresh egg noodles

1.2 litres/2 pints Vegetable stock (page 62)

2 tbsp finely chopped spring onions

1 tbsp chopped fresh coriander

115g/4oz finely chopped celery

2 tsp sesame oil

1 tbsp Chilli oil (See Tip, page 19)

2 tbsp light soy sauce

1 tbsp fresh lime juice

2 tsp sugar

1   If you are using dried noodles, cook in boiling water for 4–5 minutes. Drain, then cool in cold water. If you are using fresh noodles, blanch for 3–5 minutes in a large pan of boiling water, then immerse in cold water until needed.

2   Place the stock in a pan and bring to simmering point. Add all the remaining ingredients, except the noodles, and simmer for 5 minutes. Drain the noodles and add to the soup. Bring back to a simmer then transfer to serving bowls.

Nutrition notes per serving when dish serves 2: *567 Calories, Protein 16g, Carbohydrate 90g, Fat 19g, Saturated fat 2g, Fibre 1g, Added sugar 5g, Salt 4.75g.*

FIERY SICHUAN SOUP Ⓥ

Serves 4

55g/2oz bean thread (transparent) noodles

15g/½oz Chinese dried mushrooms

15g/½oz Chinese dried cloud ears

1 egg, beaten

2 tsp sesame oil

1.2 litres/2 pints Vegetable stock (page 62)

115g/4oz bamboo shoots, rinsed and finely shredded

1 tbsp chopped fresh root ginger

2 tbsp tomato purée

1 tbsp light soy sauce

2 tbsp dark soy sauce

2 tbsp Chilli oil (See Tip, page 19)

1 tbsp Chinese black rice vinegar or cider vinegar

2 tsp freshly ground black pepper

3 tbsp finely chopped spring onions

1   Soak the noodles in a large bowl of warm water for 15 minutes. When soft, drain and discard the water. Using scissors or a knife, cut the noodles into 7.5cm/3in lengths.

2   In separate bowls, soak the dried mushrooms and cloud ears in warm water for 20 minutes until soft. Drain the mushrooms and squeeze out any excess liquid, remove and discard stalks. Shred the mushroom caps finely. Rinse the cloud ears in cold water, drain well and leave whole. Beat together the egg and sesame oil and set aside.

3   Bring the stock to simmering point. Add the mushrooms, cloud ears, bamboo shoots, noodles and all the remaining ingredients, except the egg mixture and spring onions. Simmer for 5 minutes.

4   Just before serving, pour the egg mixture into the soup in a steady stream. Pull it into strands with a fork or chopsticks. Garnish with the spring onions.

Nutrition notes per serving: *190 Calories, Protein 6g, Carbohydrate 21g, Fat 10g, Saturated fat 2g, Fibre 1g, Added sugar 0g, Salt 2.73g.*

TIP

This hot and spicy soup, now so popular in the West, is traditionally made with pork but, when dried mushrooms and cloud ears are substituted, as they are here, it retains its excellent qualities.

CAUTION! This recipe contains lightly cooked eggs.

Starters & Appetisers

CRISPY WONTONS Ⓥ

Wontons stuffed with tasty fillings of flavourful vegetables are universally appreciated. This is a vegetarian version of the traditional Chinese treat with a filling of carrots, cabbage and beansprouts, with beancurd for body. These are delicious with hoisin sauce or, if you prefer, a dipping sauce made with your own combination of Chilli oil (See Tip, page 19), Chinese white rice vinegar and light soy sauce. They are ideal with drinks or as a starter.

Makes 30–35

1 pkt wonton skins (about 30–35)

450ml/16fl oz groundnut (peanut) oil, for deep-frying

hoisin sauce, for dipping

FOR THE FILLING

1 tbsp groundnut (peanut) oil

55g/2oz carrots, finely shredded

115g/4oz cabbage, finely shredded

55g/2oz beansprouts

2 tbsp finely chopped garlic

1 tbsp dark soy sauce

3 tbsp mashed beancurd

1 tsp sugar

½ tsp salt

1 tsp sesame oil

½ tsp freshly ground black pepper

1 Make the filling: heat a wok or large frying pan and add the oil. When moderately hot, add the carrots, cabbage, beansprouts and garlic and stir fry for 1 minute. Set aside to cool thoroughly.

2 Combine the cooled vegetables with the remaining filling ingredients and mix well. Using a teaspoon, place a small amount of filling in the centre of each wonton skin. Bring up two opposite corners, dampen the edges with a little water and pinch them together to make a triangle. Fold over the bottom two corners so they overlap, and press together. The filling should be well sealed in.

3 Heat the frying oil in a deep-fat fryer or large wok until hot. Deep-fry the filled wontons in several batches. Drain on kitchen paper, then serve with hoisin sauce.

Nutrition notes per serving when dish serves 30: *79 Calories, Protein 2g, Carbohydrate 10g, Fat 4g, Saturated fat 1g, Fibre trace, Added sugar 1g, Salt 0.32g.*

TIP

Do not make these too far ahead of time. Because they are made with a moisture-laden vegetable stuffing, the wonton skins will soften in an unpalatable way if they are allowed to stand for a long time. If possible, make and serve them straight away.

CUCUMBER NOODLE SALAD Ⓥ

Serves 2

115g/4oz bean thread (transparent) noodles

225g/8oz cucumber, peeled, halved lengthways, seeded and cut into 7.5cm/3in lengths

FOR THE DRESSING

3 tbsp light soy sauce

2 tbsp Chinese white rice vinegar or cider vinegar

2 tsp Chilli oil (See Tip)

1 tbsp sugar

1 tbsp groundnut (peanut) oil

2 tsp finely chopped fresh root ginger

3 tbsp finely chopped spring onions

1 Soak the noodles in a large bowl of very hot water for 15 minutes. Drain and immerse in cold water, then drain thoroughly in a colander. Using scissors or a knife, cut the noodles into 7.5cm/3in lengths.

2 In a large bowl, combine the dressing ingredients, then add the cucumber and noodles. Mix thoroughly. Transfer the salad to a serving plate and serve immediately or within 3 hours.

Nutrition notes per serving: *358 Calories, Protein 9g, Carbohydrate 56g, Fat 12g, Saturated fat 2g, Fibre 3g, Added sugar 8g, Salt 3.29g.*

TIP

You can buy Chilli oil or make your own. Heat a frying pan or wok over a high heat and add 150ml/¼ pint groundnut (peanut) oil. When slightly smoking, reduce the heat and add two tablespoons of chopped dried red chillies with their seeds, one tablespoon unroasted whole Sichuan peppercorns and two tablespoons of rinsed and dried whole black beans. Cook over a low heat for 10 minutes. Cool the mixture undisturbed, then pour into a jar. Stand for two days. Strain and discard the solids, return the oil to a jar with a tight-fitting lid and store indefinitely.

CRISPY NOODLE SALAD Ⓥ

Serves 4

300ml/½ pint groundnut (peanut) oil, for deep-frying

115g/4oz rice noodles, rice vermicelli or rice sticks

115g/4oz beancurd, cubed

2 garlic cloves, crushed

2 tbsp finely chopped shalloto

3 tbsp light soy sauce

1 tbsp sugar

2 tbsp Chinese white rice vinegar or cider vinegar

115g/4oz beansprouts

3 spring onions, shredded

1 fresh chilli, shredded

fresh coriander sprigs

1 Heat the oil in a deep-fat fryer or wok until moderately hot. Deep-fry the noodles until crispy and puffed up. Using a slotted spoon, remove the noodles from the oil and drain on kitchen paper. You may have to do this in batches.

2 Reheat the oil until very hot and deep-fry the beancurd cubes until golden. Remove and drain on kitchen paper.

3 For the dressing: combine the garlic, shallots, light soy sauce, sugar and Chinese white rice vinegar or cider vinegar in a small bowl and mix well. Place the crispy noodles on a serving plate and garnish with the beancurd, beansprouts, spring onions, chilli and coriander. Spoon over the dressing just before serving and mix well.

Nutrition notes per serving: *194 Calories, Protein 7g, Carbohydrate 29g, Fat 6g, Saturated fat 1g, Fibre 2g, Added sugar 4g, Salt 1.65g.*

VIETNAMESE-STYLE SPRING ROLLS Ⓥ

Makes 25 small spring rolls

1 pkt rice paper wrappers

450ml/16fl oz groundnut (peanut) oil, for deep-frying

FOR THE STUFFING

55g/2oz bean thread (transparent) noodles

55g/2oz carrots, finely shredded

115g/4oz mangetout, finely shredded

3 tbsp finely chopped spring onions

1 tsp sesame oil

2 tbsp light soy sauce

1 tsp Chinese rice wine or dry sherry

Spicy peanut sauce (recipe follows)

1 Make the stuffing: soak the noodles in a large bowl of very hot water for 15 minutes. When soft, drain and discard the water. Using scissors or a knife, cut the noodles into 7.5cm/3in lengths.

2 In a large bowl, mix the noodles with the carrots, mangetout, spring onions, sesame oil, soy sauce and rice wine or sherry.

3 Make the spring rolls: fill a large bowl with warm water and dip in one of the rice paper wrappers to soften. Remove and drain on a clean tea towel. Place about two tablespoons of filling in one corner of the wrapper. Fold over the corner to enclose the filling, then fold in each side and roll up tightly. They will seal by themselves. You should have a roll about 7.5cm/3in long, a little like a small sausage. Repeat until you have used all the filling.

4 Heat the oil in a deep-fat fryer or large wok until hot. Deep-fry the spring rolls, a few at a time, for 2 minutes or until golden brown. Drain on kitchen paper. Serve with the peanut sauce.

Nutrition notes per spring roll: *43 Calories, Protein 1g, Carbohydrate 7g, Fat 2g, Saturated fat trace, Fibre trace, Added sugar 0g, Salt 0.18g.*

TIP

Rice paper wrappers can be found in Chinese or oriental grocers. They are dry and must be gently soaked before use. Handle with care as they are quite fragile. When deep-frying the spring rolls do not crowd the pan as they tend to stick together.

SPICY PEANUT SAUCE Ⓥ

Makes enough for 25 small spring rolls

1 tbsp light soy sauce

2 tbsp Chinese white rice vinegar or cider vinegar

½ tsp finely chopped garlic

3 tbsp peanuts, skinned, roasted and coarsely chopped

1 tsp Chilli oil (See Tip, page 19)

1 tcp sugar

1 In a small bowl, combine all the ingredients with two tablespoons of water, mixing thoroughly. Leave to stand for at least 10 minutes before using.

Nutrition notes per serving: *12 Calories, Protein 1g, Carbohydrate 1g, Fat 1g, Saturated fat trace, Fibre trace, Added sugar trace, Salt 0.06g.*

CAUTION! This recipe contains nuts.

Main Courses

FRESH PASTA WITH CORIANDER, GINGER AND BASIL PESTO Ⓥ

This recipe was inspired by a colleague, Bruce Cost. A superb chef and author of excellent cookery books, one of his specialities is the food of Southeast Asia. Here, I elaborate on a version of his delicious Asian pesto. Pesto is an Italian term meaning any sauce whose ingredients have been pounded and mixed together. The original Genoan pesto sauce consists of fresh basil, Parmesan cheese, oil and garlic pounded into a smooth green paste. Combine this oriental variety of pesto with freshly made pasta or buy dried or freshly made Chinese egg noodles.

Serves 6

FOR THE PASTA

280g/10oz plain flour

3 large eggs

2 tbsp groundnut (peanut) oil

1 tsp salt

flour, for dusting

FOR THE SAUCE

1 tbsp finely chopped fresh root ginger

1 tbsp finely chopped fresh coriander

3 tbsp finely chopped fresh basil

2 tbsp finely chopped garlic

1 tbsp groundnut (peanut) oil

2 tsp sesame oil

2 tsp salt

1 tsp freshly ground black pepper

fresh basil, to garnish

1   Make the pasta by hand or in a food processor. Combine the flour, eggs, oil and salt, then knead the dough until smooth and satiny. Pass through a pasta machine twice on each setting, stopping at the thinnest setting. Cut into thin noodles. Dust lightly with flour and set aside.

2   Place all the sauce ingredients in a blender and mix thoroughly. Bring a large pan of water to the boil, add the pasta and cook for 1 minute. Drain thoroughly and toss with the sauce. Garnish with fresh basil.

Nutrition notes per serving: *269 Calories, Protein 9g, Carbohydrate 37g, Fat 10g, Saturated fat 2g, Fibre 2g, Added sugar 0g, Salt 2.58g.*

TIP

If the pasta dough is sticky once you have kneaded it, place it in the fridge to chill a little before passing it through the pasta machine. Ordinary fresh basil is used here but, if you can, try to obtain the Asian tropical variety which has a distinctive basil-anise flavour worth savouring. Fresh coriander and ginger are, of course, traditional oriental seasonings.

MINCED PORK, PEA AND RICE CASSEROLE

This is a typical Chinese dish, designed to comfort, to satisfy, to relax one's body and soul. This dish reheats very well when it is perhaps even tastier and is a meal in itself. Steaming is one of the best methods of reheating food since it warms the food without cooking it further and without drying it out. Serve with a salad and you have a splendid, complete meal.

425ml/15fl oz long grain rice

225g/8oz fresh peas (shelled weight) or frozen peas, thawed

1½ tbsp groundnut (peanut) oil

450g/1lb minced pork

1 tbsp light soy sauce

1 tbsp dark soy sauce

1 tbsp oyster sauce, plus extra, to serve (See Tip)

½ tsp salt

1 tbsp Chinese rice wine or dry sherry

3 tbsp finely chopped spring onions

1   Place the rice in a heavy pan with 850ml/1½ pints of water and bring to the boil. Continue boiling for 15–20 minutes or until most of the surface liquid has evaporated. The surface of the rice should have small indentations and look rather like a pitted crater. At this point, cover the pan with a very tight-fitting lid and reduce the heat to as low as possible.

2   If you are using fresh peas, blanch them in boiling water for 2 minutes, drain and set aside.

3   Heat a wok or large frying pan and add the oil. Add the pork and stir fry for 1 minute, then add the peas, the soy sauces, oyster sauce, salt and rice wine or sherry. Cook for 2 minutes, then add the spring onions. Place this cooked mixture on top of the rice, cover and cook over the lowest possible heat undisturbed for 15 minutes. Serve drizzled with extra oyster sauce if liked.

Nutrition notes per serving: *647 Calories, Protein 35g, Carbohydrate 100g, Fat 14g, Saturated fat 4g, Fibre 3g, Added sugar 0g, Salt 2.34g.*

TIP

Oyster sauce, which gives a rich aroma to a dish, is one of my favourite sauces for quick cooking. Thick and brown, it is made from a concentrate of oysters cooked in soy sauce, seasonings and brine. And despite its name, it does not taste fishy. It has a rich flavour and is used not only in cooking but also as a condiment, diluted with a little oil, for vegetables, poultry or meat. Look for the more expensive brands as they tend to be the highest in quality. Keep in the fridge after opening.

STIR-FRIED VEGETABLES OVER A RICE NOODLE CLOUD ⓥ

At Chinese banquets when I was a child, the food we children enjoyed most were the dishes that featured fried rice noodles. I believe this is still true today for Western children whose parents take them to Chinese restaurants. Practically any stir-fried dish with a little sauce makes a wonderful topping for these crisp, crackling, crunchy noodles. In this recipe, I combine them with slightly spiced vegetables, enhanced with aromatic seasonings.

Serves 4–6

300ml/½ pint groundnut (peanut) oil, for deep-frying

175g/6oz rice noodles, rice vermicelli or rice sticks

350g/12oz aubergines, cut into 7.5cm/3in lengths (See Tip)

225g/8oz courgettes, cut into 7.5cm/3in lengths

3 garlic cloves, crushed

4 spring onions, chopped

2 tbsp Chinese rice wine or dry sherry

2 tbsp yellow bean sauce

2 tsp chilli bean sauce

150ml/¼ pint Vegetable stock (page 62)

1 tsp sugar

2 tbsp dark soy sauce

1 tsp salt, plus extra for salting vegetables

1 tsp cornflour mixed with 1 tsp water

1 Heat the oil in a deep-fat fryer or large wok until very hot. Deep-fry the noodles until crisp and puffed up. Using a slotted spoon, remove the noodles from the oil and drain on kitchen paper. You may have to do this in batches.

2 Meanwhile, place the aubergine and courgette lengths in a sieve set over a bowl and sprinkle with salt. Leave to drain for 20 minutes, rinse under cold running water and pat dry with kitchen paper.

3 Heat a wok or large frying pan and add one and a half tablespoons of the oil in which you have fried the noodles. When moderately hot, add the garlic and spring onions and stir fry for 30 seconds.

4 Add the aubergines and courgettes and stir fry for 1 minute. Stir in all the remaining ingredients, except for the cornflour mixture, and cook for 3 minutes. Stir in the blended cornflour and cook for 1 minute. Place the deep-fried noodles on serving plates and spoon over the vegetables.

Nutrition notes per serving when dish serves 4: *296 Calories, Protein 5g, Carbohydrate 47g, Fat 10g, Saturated fat 2g, Fibre 3g, Added sugar 3.8g, Salt 3.34g.*

TIP

Aubergines, also known as eggplants, are smooth and purple-skinned. They range in size from the huge fat ones which are easy to find to the small thin variety which the Chinese prefer because they have a more delicate flavour. The Chinese do not normally peel aubergines, since the skin preserves their texture, shape and taste. The salting process extracts excess moisture and bitter juices from the vegetable before it is cooked.

HOT AND SOUR NOODLES Ⓥ

Serves 4

450g/1lb dried or fresh egg noodles

1 tbsp sesame oil

FOR THE SAUCE

2 tbsp dark soy sauce

1 tbsp Chilli oil (See Tip, page 19)

1 tbsp Chinese black rice vinegar or cider vinegar

3 tbsp finely chopped spring onions

¼ tsp freshly ground black pepper

1 tsp sugar

1 If you are using dried noodles, cook for 4–5 minutes in a large pan of boiling water, If you are using fresh noodles, cook for 3–5 minutes in boiling water. Drain, toss in the sesame oil, then set aside.

2 Place all the sauce ingredients in a small pan and heat together over a low heat for 5 minutes until the spring onions have softened.

3 Bring a pan of water to the boil and plunge the noodles in for 20 seconds, then drain well in a sieve or colander. Tip into a large bowl, pour over the sauce and mix together well.

Nutrition notes per serving: *503 Calories, Protein 14g, Carbohydrate 84g, Fat 15g, Saturated fat 1g, Fibre 3g, Added sugar 1g, Salt 1.61g.*

HOT AND SPICY RICE WITH BEEF

Serves 4–6

425ml/15fl oz long grain rice

4 tbsp groundnut (peanut) oil

2 tsp salt

450g/1lb minced beef

2 tbsp coarsely chopped garlic

1 tbsp coarsely chopped fresh root ginger

2 tsp chilli bean sauce

1 tsp curry paste or powder

3 tbsp coarsely chopped spring onions

1 Place the rice in a heavy pan with 850ml/1½ pints water and bring to the boil. Continue boiling for 15–20 minutes or until most of the surface liquid has evaporated. The surface of the rice should have small indentations and look rather like a pitted crater. At this point, cover the pan with a very tight fitting lid and reduce the heat to as low as possible. Cook the rice, undisturbed, for 15 minutes more. Remove from the heat and leave to go cold. The colder the rice, the better it stir fries.

2 Heat a wok or large frying pan and add half the oil and all the salt. Add the beef and stir fry for 4 minutes, stirring well to break up any clumps of meat. Remove the beef from the wok and set aside. Drain the oil from the wok.

3 Reheat the wok and add the remaining oil, then add the garlic, ginger, chilli bean sauce and curry paste or powder and stir fry for 30 seconds. Add the cold cooked rice and beef and spring onions and stir fry for 5 minutes. Serve at once or cool and serve at room temperature.

Nutrition notes per serving when dish serves 4: *695 Calories, Protein 31g, Carbohydrate 94g, Fat 24g, Saturated fat 7g, Fibre 1g, Added sugar 0g, Salt 2.74g.*

TIP

Speed up the preparation by boiling the rice in advance. Store, well covered, in the fridge until needed. You could use the leftover rice from making a Rice Cake (page 12) to make a speedy half quantity of this dish to serve two.

SPICY RICE NOODLES WITH MUSSELS

Fish and shellfish by their very nature are best when not overcooked and the sweet succulent sea flavours are retained through careful and quick cooking. I think no other cuisine matches that of the Chinese in its ability to capture the best flavours and textures of the harvest of the sea. This dish is useful for entertaining a large group of friends at short notice. Only the careful cleaning of the mussels takes any time; the rest of the preparation is very quick. You can substitute prawns or clams for the mussels, but whatever seafood you use it will result in a tasty and substantial dish that makes a complete and satisfying meal.

Serves 4–6

225g/8oz rice noodles, rice vermicelli or rice sticks

2 tbsp groundnut (peanut) oil

1 tbsp black beans, left whole

2 tbsp coarsely chopped garlic

2 tbsp coarsely chopped spring onions

900g/2lb fresh mussels, well scrubbed and beards removed (See Tip)

1 tbsp Chinese rice wine or dry sherry

1 tbsp yellow bean sauce

2 tbsp chilli bean sauce

1 Bring a large pan of water to the boil, remove from the heat and add the rice noodles. Stand for 15 minutes, then drain well in a sieve or colander.

2 Heat a wok or large frying pan and add the oil, black beans, garlic and spring onions. Stir fry for 20 seconds, then add the mussels, rice wine or sherry, yellow bean sauce and chilli bean sauce. Cook for 5 minutes or until all the mussels have opened. Discard any remain closed.

3 Add the rice noodles to the wok or frying pan and cook for 2 minutes until heated through, mixing well. Give the dish a final stir before serving.

Nutrition notes per serving when dish serves 4: *301 Calories, Protein 12g, Carbohydrate 50g, Fat 7g, Saturated fat 1g, Fibre 1g, Added sugar 1g, Salt 0.65g.*

TIP

Make sure that your mussels are really fresh when buying them and are firmly closed before cooking. Throw away any that do not shut when tapped lightly or that have damaged shells. You can now buy mussels already scrubbed and cleaned in many large supermarkets.

STIR-FRIED SCALLOPS WITH ASPARAGUS AND MANGETOUT

Scallops are fragile, sweetly delicate morsels and need very little preparation or cooking time. In this recipe I combine them with the subtle flavours of asparagus and mangetout. This dish is perfect for a family meal or as the centrepiece for a dinner party as it doesn't take too long to prepare.

Serves 4

225g/8oz rice noodles, rice vermicelli or rice sticks

450g/1lb fresh scallops, including the corals (See Tip)

1½ tbsp groundnut oil

1½ tbsp coarsely chopped spring onions

1 tbsp coarsely chopped garlic

1 tbsp finely chopped fresh root ginger

225g/8oz fresh asparagus, trimmed and cut diagonally into 2.5cm/1 in pieces

115g/4oz mangetout, trimmed and cut in half

FOR THE SAUCE

1 tbsp light soy sauce

2 tsp yellow bean sauce

2 tbsp Chinese rice wine or dry sherry

1 tsp sugar

1 tsp sesame oil

1 Bring a a large pan of water to the boil, remove from the heat and add the rice noodles. Leave to stand for 15 minutes. Meanwhile, wash the scallops, pat dry with kitchen paper and set aside.

2 Heat a wok or large frying pan until hot and then add the oil. Add the spring onions, garlic and ginger and stir fry for 30 seconds then add the asparagus and stir fry for 2 minutes. Stir in the scallops, mangetout and all the sauce ingredients and cook for 4 minutes.

3 Drain the rice noodles well in a sieve or colander. Place in a warm serving dish and spoon over the scallops and vegetables with their sauces.

Nutrition notes per serving: *374 Calories, Protein 28g, Carbohydrate 52g, Fat 7g, Saturated fat 1g, Fibre 2g, Added sugar 2g, Salt 1.29g.*

TIP

Mussels or clams may be substituted for the scallops, and red and green peppers or courgettes could also be substituted for the asparagus and mangetout. If you like spicy food, add two finely sliced fresh chillies. Buy fresh cleaned scallops out of their shells and avoid frozen ones which are often lacking in taste.

RICE WITH CHINESE SAUSAGE

Serves 4-6

425ml/15fl oz long grain rice

350g/12oz Chinese sausages, cut diagonally into 5cm/2in chunks

1   Place the rice in a heavy pan with 850ml/1½ pints of water and bring to the boil. Continue boiling for 15–20 minutes or until most of the surface liquid has evaporated. By now the surface should have small indentations and look rather like a pitted crater.

2   At this point, place the sausages on top of the rice, cover the pan with a very tight-fitting lid, reduce the heat to as low as possible and let the rice cook undisturbed for 15 minutes more.

Nutrition notes per serving when dish serves 4: *667 Calories, Protein 23g, Carbohydrate 93g, Fat 25g, Saturated fat 9g, Fibre 0g, Added sugar 0g, Salt 2.91g.*

CHOW MEIN Ⓥ

Serves 4

225g/8oz dried or fresh egg noodles

2 tbsp groundnut (peanut) oil

4 garlic cloves, crushed

2 tsp finely chopped fresh root ginger

1 small onion, finely sliced

175g/6oz small button mushrooms, sliced

55g/2oz celery, diagonally sliced

55g/2oz canned bamboo shoots, drained and shredded

1 tbsp light soy sauce

2 tbsp dark soy sauce

3 tbsp Vegetable stock (page 62)

1 tbsp Chinese rice wine or dry sherry

1 tsp sugar

115g/4oz beansprouts

fresh coriander sprigs, to garnish

1   If you are using dried noodles, cook for 4–5 minutes in a large pan of boiling water, If you are using fresh noodles, cook for 3–5 minutes in boiling water. Drain, then place in cold water until needed.

2   Heat a wok or large frying pan and add the oil. When moderately hot, add the garlic and ginger and stir fry for 10 seconds. Add the onion and fry to soften. Add the mushrooms, then the celery and bamboo shoots and stir fry for 5 minutes.

3   Drain the noodles thoroughly and add to the wok. Stir fry for 1 minute, then add all the remaining ingredients, except the beansprouts and coriander, Add the stock as required if the mixture begins to dry out. Stir fry for 2 minutes, then stir in the beansprouts. Give the mixture a good stir, transfer to serving plates and garnish with coriander sprigs.

Nutrition notes per serving: *316 Calories, Protein 10g, Carbohydrate 47g, Fat 11g, Saturated fat 1g, Fibre 3g, Added sugar 1g, Salt 1.96g.*

TIP

Chow mein can be kept warm for at least 1 hour without losing any of its charm; I enjoy it cold. Serve as an economical family meal or at a buffet party.

CRISPY CANTONESE-STYLE NOODLES WITH VEGETABLES Ⓥ

The origins of pasta are obscured by time and controversy, but there is a general consensus that the Chinese first thought of the egg noodle variety. Whoever invented the process, pan-fried noodles make a perfect foundation for stir-fried dishes. Here, the pan-frying technique leaves the noodles brown, firm and crispy on the outside and yellow, moist and soft on the inside, a combination of textures that is classically Chinese. Upon this noodle base are placed stir-fried vegetables topped with a zesty sauce.

Serves 2–4

225g/8oz dried or fresh thin Chinese egg noodles

2 tbsp groundnut (peanut) oil

4 garlic cloves, lightly crushed

1 tsp salt

55g/2oz celery, coarsely chopped

115g/4oz red pepper, finely shredded

25g/1oz button mushrooms, finely shredded

115g/4oz mangetout, trimmed (See Tip)

6 spring onions, finely shredded

300ml/½ pint Vegetable stock (page 62)

2 tsp cornflour mixed with 2 tsp water

3 tbsp Chinese rice wine or dry sherry

2 tsp light soy sauce

2 tbsp dark soy sauce

1 tsp chilli bean sauce

shredded spring onions, to garnish

1   If you are using dried noodles, cook according to packet instructions, or boil for 2 minutes until soft. If you are using fresh Chinese egg noodles, boil for 3 minutes, then drain thoroughly. Scatter on a baking tray.

2   Heat a large non-stick frying pan and add half the oil. When hot, add the noodles and press down to make the noodles conform to the shape of the pan. Turn the heat to very low, and cook for 10–15 minutes until brown. Flip the noodles over in one piece and continue cooking until the other side is brown. You may have to add a little oil or water from time to time to keep the noodles moist.

3   Meanwhile, heat a wok or large frying pan until hot. Add the remaining oil, the garlic and salt and stir fry for a few seconds. Stir in the celery, red pepper and mushrooms and stir fry for 3 minutes. Add the mangetout and spring onions and stir fry for 2 minutes.

4   Stir in the stock and bring to the boil. Add the cornflour and stir until the sauce is cooked through and thickened. Add the rice wine or sherry, soy sauces and chilli bean sauce. Place the noodles on serving plates, then pour over the vegetables and sauce. Garnish with spring onions.

Nutrition notes per serving when dish serves 2: *279 Calories, Protein 8g, Carbohydrate 34g, Fat 12g, Saturated fat 2g, Fibre 4g, Added sugar trace, Salt 5.98g.*

TIP

Mangetout combine a crisp texture with a sweet, fresh flavour. Look for pods that are firm with very small peas, which means they will be tender and young. They will keep for a week in the vegetable compartment of the fridge.

JAPANESE RICE WITH ASPARAGUS Ⓥ

425ml/15fl oz short grain rice

700ml/1¼ pints Vegetable stock (page 62)

2 tbsp light soy sauce

1 tbsp dark soy sauce

150ml/¼ pint Japanese sake, Chinese rice wine or dry sherry

2 tbsp groundnut (peanut) oil

450g/1lb fresh asparagus, trimmed and cut diagonally into 7.5cm/3in long pieces

¼ tsp salt

2 tbsp finely shredded fresh root ginger

1 Place the rice in a heavy pan with the stock, soy sauces and sake and bring to the boil. Continue boiling for 15–20 minutes or until most of the surface liquid has evaporated. By now the surface should have small indentations and look rather like a pitted crater. At this point, cover the pan with a very tight-fitting lid, reduce the heat to as low as possible and let the rice cook undisturbed for 15–20 minutes.

2 Heat a wok or large frying pan and add the oil. Stir in the asparagus pieces and salt and stir fry for 4 minutes. Remove the asparagus from the pan and cool slightly. Fold the asparagus into the warm cooked rice with the ginger.

Nutrition notes per serving when dish serves 2: *1040 Calories, Protein 22g, Carbohydrate 195g, Fat 15g, Saturated fat 3g, Fibre 5g, Added sugar 1g, Salt 5.09g.*

TIP

Asparagus is expensive even when in season, but it is so exquisite a treat it is worth buying as often as you can. Properly cooked, it has a firm but soft texture, a delicate earthy, assertive flavour and a brilliant colour. You can substitute broccoli or runner beans if you prefer.

BEAN SAUCE NOODLES

225g/8oz flat rice noodles

1 tbsp light soy sauce

2 tsp sesame oil

1 tbsp groundnut (peanut) oil

350g/12oz minced pork

5 tbsp yellow bean sauce

2 tsp sugar

6 spring onions, coarsely chopped

1 Bring a large pan of water to the boil, remove from the heat and add the rice noodles. Stand for 15 minutes, then drain and toss with the soy sauce and sesame oil.

2 Heat a work or large frying pan and add the groundnut oil, then the pork. Stir fry for 2 minutes, breaking up any clumps of meat, then add the yellow bean sauce and sugar and cook for 3 minutes. Stir in the spring onions. Place the noodles on serving plates and spoon over the sauce.

Nutrition notes per serving when dish serves 4: *398 Calories, Protein 22g, Carbohydrate 56g, Fat 11g, Saturated fat 3g, Fibre 1g, Added sugar 9g, Salt 1.38g.*

KOREAN BEAN THREAD SESAME NOODLES AND VEGETABLES Ⓥ

This simple-to-prepare recipe is my own version of a popular Korean dish. What makes it memorable is the combination of lace-like noodles and exotic mushrooms, an unusual mixture of tastes and textures.

Serves 4

25g/1oz Chinese dried mushrooms

15g/½oz Chinese dried cloud ears

115g/4oz bean thread (transparent) noodles

2 tbsp groundnut (peanut) oil

55g/2oz carrot, finely shredded

1 small onion, fincly shredded

1 green pepper, finely shredded

FOR THE SAUCE

2 tbsp light soy sauce

2 tbsp dark soy sauce

3 tbsp sesame oil

1½ tbsp sesame seeds (See Tip)

1 tbsp finely chopped garlic

1 tbsp sugar

1 tsp freshly ground black pepper

1 Soak the dried mushrooms in warm water for 20 minutes until soft. Squeeze out any excess liquid, remove and discard the stalks. Cut the caps into shreds. Soak the cloud ears in warm water for 20 minutes or until soft. Rinse well in cold water and drain thoroughly in a colander. Leave whole.

2 Soak the noodles in a large bowl of very hot water for 15 minutes. When soft, drain well. Using scissors or a knife, cut the noodles into 7.5cm/3in lengths.

3 Heat a work or large frying pan and add the oil. When moderately hot, add the mushrooms, cloud ears, carrot, onion, green pepper and 125ml/4fl oz of water and stir fry for 5 minutes or until the carrots are cooked.

4 Combine the sauce ingredients and add to the vegetables. Give the mixture a good stir, then add the noodles. Stir fry the mixture for 2 minutes until heated through. Serve at once or at room temperature.

Nutrition notes per serving: *347 Calories, Protein 7g, Carbohydrate 39g, Fat 19g, Saturated fat 3g, Fibre 3g, Added sugar 4g, Salt 2.21g.*

TIP

Sesame seeds are the dried seeds of an oriental annual herb. Unhulled, the seeds range from greyish white to black in colour, but once the hull is removed, the sesame seeds are flat, tiny, creamy coloured, and pointed at one end. They are valued as a flavouring agent and as a source of oil and paste. Kept in a glass jar in a cool, dry place, they will last indefinitely.

SINGAPORE-STYLE RICE NOODLES Ⓥ

This dish is just such a treat. Rice noodles are lighter than wheat noodles and therefore blend perfectly with the vegetables and curry sauce. This is equally delicious warm or cold.

Serves 2–4

225g/8oz flat rice noodles

2 eggs, beaten

2 tsp sesame oil

1½ tsp salt

2 tbsp groundnut (peanut) oil

115g/4oz carrots, finely shredded

115g/4oz leeks, white part only, finely shredded

4 spring onions, finely shredded

115g/4oz red pepper, finely shredded

25g/1oz fresh chillies, finely shredded

fresh coriander leaves, to garnish

FOR THE CURRY SAUCE

2 tbsp curry paste

1 tbsp finely chopped garlic

1 tbsp finely chopped fresh root ginger

300ml/½ pint Vegetable stock (page 62)

1 tbsp sugar

2 tbsp Chinese rice wine or dry sherry

2 tbsp light soy sauce

1 Soak the rice noodles in a bowl of warm water for 25 minutes. Drain in a colander. In a small bowl, combine the eggs with the sesame oil and half a teaspoon of the salt.

2 Heat a wok or large frying pan over a high heat and add the oil. When almost smoking, add the carrots, leeks, spring onions and remaining salt and stir fry for a few seconds. Add the red pepper and chillies and stir fry for 1 minute.

3 Stir in the curry sauce ingredients and the drained noodles. Stir fry for 5 minutes until well mixed and heated through. Add the egg mixture, blending thoroughly. Stir fry for 1 minute, then garnish with fresh coriander.

Nutrition notes per serving when dish serves 2: *730 Calories, Protein 17g, Carbohydrate 115g, Fat 24g, Saturated fat 4g, Fibre 8g, Added sugar 8g, Salt 7.22g.*

TIP

Curry paste has a stronger curry flavour than powder. The spices are mixed with oil and chilli peppers. Be sure to get the Indian variety which is generally the best. Keep chilled after opening.

CAUTION! This recipe contains lightly cooked eggs.

Cold Dishes & Salads

SPICY BLACK BEAN NOODLES Ⓥ

Ever since I can remember, the aroma of black beans cooked with garlic has meant mouth-watering food. Because I enjoy cold noodles, I have adapted these seasonings for a light lunch dish or accompaniment for summer evening meals. The pungent sauce is cooked in advance and allowed to cool before enlivening the cold noodles.

Serves 2

350g/12oz dried or fresh Chinese egg noodles

FOR THE SAUCE

3 tbsp groundnut (peanut) oil

2 tbsp yellow bean sauce

2 tbsp black beans, rinsed and coarsely chopped (See Tip)

2 tbsp finely chopped garlic

1 tbsp finely chopped fresh root ginger

2 tbsp finely chopped spring onions

2 tsp chilli bean sauce

2 tsp sugar

1 tbsp dark soy sauce

2 tsp Chilli oil (See Tip, page 19)

2 tbsp Chinese rice wine or dry sherry

150ml/¼ pint Vegetable stock (page 62)

1 tsp cornflour mixed with 1 tsp water

1 If you are using dried noodles, cook in a large pan of boiling water for 4–5 minutes. If you are using fresh noodles, blanch in boiling water for 3–5 minutes. Drain, then place in cold water until required.

2 Make the sauce: heat a wok or large frying pan and add the oil. When moderately hot, add the yellow bean sauce, black beans, garlic, ginger and spring onions and stir fry for 2 minutes.

3 Add all the remaining ingredients, except the cornflour mixture, and cook for 2 minutes. Stir in the blended cornflour and bring to the boil for 30 seconds. Remove from the heat and allow to cool. Drain the noodles thoroughly in a colander and mix with the sauce.

Nutrition notes per serving: 980 Calories, Protein 25g, Carbohydrate 147g, Fat 35g, Saturated fat 4g, Fibre 7g, Added sugar 10g, Salt 2.81g.

TIP

Black beans are small black soya beans and are also known as salted black beans. They are preserved by being fermented with salt and spices. They have a distinctive, slightly salty taste and a pleasantly rich smell, and are used as a seasoning, often in conjunction with garlic and fresh ginger. Black beans are inexpensive and can be found in tins as 'black beans in salted sauce'. You may also see them packed in plastic bags, which are preferable. Rinse before use; I prefer to chop the beans slightly, too. Transfer any unused beans and liquid to a sealed jar and keep in the fridge.

SWEETCORN AND GINGER FRIED RICE ⓥ

425ml/15fl oz long grain rice

1 tbsp groundnut (peanut) oil

1½ tsp finely chopped fresh root ginger

2 tbsp finely chopped spring onions

2 tbsp Chinese rice wine or dry sherry

450g/1lb fresh sweetcorn on the cob, kernels removed, or 280g/10oz canned sweetcorn, drained

½ tsp salt

¼ tsp freshly ground black pepper

2 tbsp sesame oil

1 Place the rice in a heavy pan with 750ml/1½ pints of water and bring to the boil. Continue boiling for 15–20 minutes or until most of the surface liquid has evaporated. By now the surface should have small indentations and look rather like a pitted crater. At this point, cover the pan with a very tight-fitting lid, reduce the heat to as low as possible and let the rice cook undisturbed for 15–20 minutes. Leave to go cold.

2 Heat a wok or large frying pan and add the oil. Add the ginger and spring onions and stir fry for a few seconds. Add the rice wine or sherry and stir fry for a few more seconds.

3 Stir in the cold cooked rice and stir fry for 5 minutes, then add the corn, salt and pepper and stir fry for 2 minutes. Add the sesame oil and stir fry for 4 minutes until the corn is thoroughly cooked.

Nutrition notes per serving: *556 Calories, Protein 9g, Carbohydrate 112g, Fat 10g, Saturated fat 1g, Fibre 1g, Added sugar 5g, Salt 1.12g.*

TIP

Use fresh corn if possible, and be sure the cooked rice is really cold before stir frying. This will keep it from absorbing too much oil and becoming sticky. This economical and healthy dish may be eaten as a rice salad or as a delicious vegetable accompaniment.

ELIZABETH CHONG'S NOODLE SALAD ⓥ

175g/6oz bean thread (transparent) noodles

1 tbsp groundnut (peanut) oil

2 tsp salt

350g/12oz beansprouts

6 spring onions, finely shredded

1½ tsp chilli bean sauce

1½ tbsp Chinese white rice vinegar

1 tbsp light soy sauce

2 tsp sesame oil

shredded spring onions, to garnish

1 Soak the noodles in a large bowl of warm water for 15 minutes. When soft, drain well. Using scissors or a knife, cut the noodles into 7.5cm/3in lengths.

2 Heat a wok or large frying pan and add the oil, salt, beansprouts and spring onions and stir fry for 10 seconds. Add the chilli bean sauce, Chinese white rice vinegar, soy sauce, sesame oil and noodles and cook for 1 minute. Cool, then keep, covered, in the fridge. Garnish with spring onions before serving.

Nutrition notes per serving when dish serves 4: *244 Calories, Protein 8g, Carbohydrate 38g, Fat 8g, Saturated fat 1g, Fibre 3g, Added sugar 1g, Salt 3.10g.*

GREEN RICE ⓥ

Serves 4–6

425ml/15fl oz long grain rice

225g/8oz fresh peas (shelled weight) or frozen peas, thawed

1 tbsp groundnut (peanut) oil

1 tbsp coarsely chopped garlic

3 tbsp finely chopped fresh coriander

6 tbsp finely chopped spring onions

2 tsp salt

1 Place the rice in a heavy pan with 750ml/1½ pints of water and bring to the boil. Continue boiling for 15–20 minutes or until most of the surface liquid has evaporated. By now the surface should have small indentations and look rather like a pitted crater. At this point, cover the pan with a very tight-fitting lid, reduce the heat to as low as possible and let the rice cook undisturbed for 15 minutes. Leave to go cold. The colder the rice, the better it stir fries.

2 If you are using fresh peas, blanch them in boiling water for 2 minutes, then drain and set aside.

3 Heat a wok or large frying pan, then add the oil. Add the garlic and stir for 10 seconds. Add the cold rice and stir fry for 3 minutes. Stir in the coriander, spring onions, peas and salt and stir fry for 2 minutes. Serve at once or cool and serve at room temperature.

Nutrition notes per serving when dish serves 4: 463 Calories, Protein 12g, Carbohydrate 100g, Fat 5g, Saturated fat 1g, Fibre 3g, Added sugar 0g, Salt 2.49g.

COLD SICHUAN NOODLES ⓥ

Serves 2

450g/1lb dried or fresh Chinese egg noodles

2 tbsp groundnut (peanut) oil

2 tbsp finely chopped spring onions

1 tbsp finely chopped garlic

1 tbsp yellow bean sauce

2 tsp chilli bean sauce

2 tsp finely chopped fresh root ginger

1 tbsp Chinese rice wine or dry sherry

2 tbsp dark soy sauce

2 tbsp sesame oil

fresh coriander leaves, to garnish

1 If using dried noodles, cook according to packet instructions or boil for 4–5 minutes. Cool in cold water until needed. If using fresh noodles, boil for 3–5 minutes, then immerse in cold water.

2 Heat a wok or large frying pan and add the oil. When hot, add the spring onions, garlic, yellow bean sauce, chilli bean sauce and ginger and stir fry for 2 minutes. Remove from the heat and cool thoroughly.

3 Drain the noodles and combine with the cooled seasonings, the rice wine or sherry, soy sauce and sesame oil. Garnish with coriander and serve within 3 hours.

Nutrition notes per serving: 1126 Calories, Protein 29g, Carbohydrate 169g, Fat 41g, Saturated fat 4g, Fibre 7g, Added sugar 3g, Salt 3.47g.

TIP

This makes an ideal lunch dish for two, but the portions may be increased easily for use in a family meal.

SOUTHEAST ASIA NOODLE SALAD Ⓥ

On my first visit to Southeast Asia many years ago, what most impressed me was the use of exotic and fascinating combinations of ingredients such as coconut milk, limes, fish sauce and herbs, such as basil, all of which were foreign to my tradition. I have since become familiar with these and other once strange ingredients, and my experiments have led me to some very delectable results, as with this light lunch or supper noodle dish, which includes an aromatic combination of splendid tastes and colours.

Serves 4

225g/8oz flat rice noodles

2 spring onions, finely shredded

55g/2oz mangetout, finely shredded

55g/2oz carrot, finely shredded

115g/4oz beansprouts

3 tbsp peanuts, skinned, roasted and coarsely chopped, to garnish

FOR THE DRESSING

2 tbsp fresh lime juice

2 tsp Chilli oil (See Tip, page 19)

2 tbsp light soy sauce

2 tsp sesame oil

1 tbsp fresh lemon juice

6 tbsp canned coconut milk (See Tip)

½ tsp salt

grated rind of 1 lime

½ tsp freshly ground black pepper

1 tbsp sugar

2 tbsp finely chopped fresh coriander

1½ tbsp finely chopped fresh root ginger

4 tbsp finely chopped fresh basil

1   Bring a large pan of water to the boil, remove from the heat and add the rice noodles. Stand for 15 minutes. Drain, then immerse in cold water.

2   Bring a pan of water to the boil and blanch the spring onions, mangetout, carrot and beansprouts for 1 minute. Immerse immediately in cold water, drain and set aside.

3   Combine all the dressing ingredients. Drain the noodles thoroughly and toss them with the dressing and vegetables. Garnish with the peanuts and serve within 3 hours.

Nutrition notes per serving: *326 Calories, Protein 8g, Carbohydrate 57g, Fat 9g, Saturated fat 2g, Fibre 2g, Added sugar 4g, Salt 1.81g.*

TIP

I find canned coconut milk quite acceptable and a lot less work than making fresh. Look for the ones from Thailand or Malaysia. Shake the tins well before opening. Transfer any remaining to a jug, cover and place in the fridge where it will keep for at least a week.

CAUTION! This recipe contains nuts.

Side Dishes

PINEAPPLE FRIED RICE ⓥ

I first enjoyed this unusual rice dish in Hong Kong and only subsequently learned of its Thai origin. Thai cooks commonly hollow out the pineapple and fill it with fried rice or some other tasty stuffing. It is a very attractive way to serve fried rice, but hollowing out the fruit takes a little effort and is not to be done every day. This is a great dish for a dinner party.

Serves 4–6

425ml/15fl oz long grain rice

1 large fresh pineapple

25g/1oz Chinese dried mushrooms

2 tbsp groundnut (peanut) oil

1 small onion, finely chopped

115g/4oz Chinese long beans, runner beans or French beans, trimmed and diced (See Tip)

2 eggs

2 tbsp dark soy sauce

1 tbsp light soy sauce

1   Place the rice in a heavy pan with 750ml/1½ pints of water and bring to the boil. Continue boiling for 15 20 minutes or until most of the surface liquid has evaporated. By now the surface should have small indentations and look rather like a pitted crater. At this point, cover the pan with a very tight-fitting lid, reduce the heat to as low as possible and let the rice cook undisturbed for 15 minutes. Leave to go cold. The colder the rice, the better it stir fries.

2   If you want to use the whole shell for serving, carefully cut off and save the pineapple top, leaving about 2.5cm/1in of the pineapple under the leaves. Alternatively, cut the pineapple in half lengthways. Scoop out the inside fruit, leaving the outer shell of the pineapple intact. Coarsely chop the pineapple flesh, discarding the tough core.

3   Soak the dried mushrooms in warm water for 20 minutes until soft. Squeeze out any excess liquid, remove and discard stalks. Cut the caps into small dice.

4   Heat a wok or large frying pan and add the oil. When almost smoking, add the mushrooms, onion and beans and stir fry for 1 minute. Mix in the cold cooked rice and stir fry for 1 minute. Add the eggs and soy sauces and stir fry for 5 minutes over a high heat.

5   Stir in the chopped pineapple flesh and stir fry for 2 minutes. Spoon the mixture into the hollowed-out pineapple shells and replace the top, or pile the mixture into the two halves, and serve the remaining rice in a dish.

Nutrition notes per serving when dish serves 4: *597 Calories, Protein 16g, Carbohydrate 112g, Fat 13g, Saturated fat 3g, Fibre 2g, Added sugar 0g, Salt 1.84g.*

TIP

Chinese long beans are also known as yard-long beans as they can grow to a yard (about a metre) in length. Although runner beans and French beans can be substituted for long beans, they are not related, the long beans having originated in Asia. Buy beans that are fresh and bright green, with no dark marks. You will usually find them sold in looped bunches. Store in a plastic bag in the fridge and use within four days.

FRAGRANT COCONUT RICE ⓥ

Serves 4

2 tbsp groundnut (peanut) oil

175g/6oz onions, chopped

425ml/15fl oz long grain or 'easy-cook' rice (See Tip)

1 tsp turmeric

2 tsp salt

425ml can coconut milk

150ml/¼ pint Vegetable stock (page 62)

2 whole cloves

1 whole cinnamon stick or Chinese cinnamon bark

2 bay leaves

1 Heat the oil in a large flameproof casserole until moderately hot. Add the onions and stir fry for 2 minutes. Stir in the rice, turmeric and salt, and cook for 2 minutes.

2 Pour in the coconut milk and stock and bring to the boil. Stir in the cloves, cinnamon and bay leaves. Reduce the heat to as low as possible and cook the rice undisturbed for 20 minutes. It is ready to serve when the rice is cooked.

Nutrition notes per serving: *476 Calories, Protein 8g, Carbohydrate 102g, Fat 7g, Saturated fat 1g, Fibre 1g, Added sugar 0g, Salt 2.91g.*

TIP

For this recipe, you may use 'easy-cook' rice. Because of the richness and oil in the coconut used, this is one of those rare dishes in which such pre-cooked rice works well. Unusual as the combination of spices may seem, you will find them a harmonious blend with this dish. If you use long grain rice it will be a little sticky, as it should be. The rice reheats well but should be warmed over a very low heat.

SINGAPORE-STYLE LETTUCE FRIED RICE ⓥ

Serves 4

425ml/15fl oz long grain rice

15g/½oz Chinese dried mushrooms

2 tbsp groundnut (peanut) oil

4 shallots, sliced

3 garlic cloves, crushed

55g/2oz fresh or frozen peas

3 tbsp finely chopped spring onions

2 fresh chillies, finely shredded

2 eggs, beaten

3 tbsp light soy sauce

½ tsp salt

¼ tsp freshly ground black pepper

225g/8oz iceberg lettuce, finely shredded

2 tbsp finely chopped spring onions, to garnish

1 Place the rice in a heavy pan with 750ml/1½ pints of water and bring to the boil. Continue boiling for 15–20 minutes or until most of the surface liquid has evaporated. By now the surface should have small indentations and look rather like a pitted crater. At this point, cover the pan with a very tight-fitting lid, reduce the heat to as low as possible and let the rice cook undisturbed for 15 minutes. Leave to go cold. The colder the rice, the better it stir fries.

2 Soak the dried mushrooms in warm water for 20 minutes until soft. Squeeze out any excess liquid, remove and discard stalks. Cut the caps into small dice.

3 Heat a wok or large frying pan and add the oil. When almost smoking, add the shallots and garlic and stir fry for 30 seconds. Add the cold cooked rice and stir fry for 1 minute, then add the peas, spring onions and chillies and stir fry for 3 minutes.

4 Stir in the beaten eggs, soy sauce, salt and pepper and stir fry for 2 minutes or until the eggs have set. Add the lettuce and mix thoroughly. Turn the mixture on to a serving plate and garnish with the spring onions.

Nutrition notes per serving: *517 Calories, Protein 13g, Carbohydrate 100g, Fat 10g, Saturated fat 2g, Fibre 2g, Added sugar 0g, Salt 2.37g.*

SPICY CITRUS-FLAVOURED NOODLES Ⓥ

Serves 2–4

225g/8oz dried or fresh Chinese egg noodles

1 tbsp sesame oil

FOR THE SAUCE

1 dried red chilli

grated rind of 1 lemon and 1 orange

2 tsp groundnut (peanut) oil

2 tsp sesame paste (See Tip)

2 tbsp each of fresh orange juice and fresh lemon juice

1 tsp finely chopped spring onions

1 tsp finely chopped garlic

1 tbsp Chinese white rice vinegar or cider vinegar

1 tbsp dark soy sauce

2 tsp sugar

¼ tsp Sichuan peppercorns

2 tsp Chilli oil (See Tip, page 19)

1   If using dried noodles, cook according to packet instructions or boil for 4–5 minutes. Cool in cold water until required. If using fresh noodles, boil for 3–5 minutes, then immerse in cold water. In the same hot water, blanch the dried chilli until soft, then blanch the citrus rinds for 30 seconds to remove their bitterness. Drain well.

2   Make the sauce: mix together all the sauce ingredients, with the chilli and citrus rinds, in a bowl or in a blender. Drain the cooked noodles, toss them with the sesame oil and transfer to a plate or bowl. Toss the noodles well with the sauce just before serving.

Nutrition notes per serving when dish serves 2: *622 Calories, Protein 16g, Carbohydrate 91g, Fat 24g, Saturated fat 3g, Fibre trace, Added sugar 6g, Salt 1.72g.*

TIP

The sauce can be made in advance and kept chilled, as it is served cold. If you prefer you can use smooth peanut butter instead of the sesame paste.

THAI AROMATIC FRIED RICE Ⓥ

Serves 4

425ml/15fl oz long grain rice

2 tbsp groundnut (peanut) oil

115g/4oz onions, finely chopped

¼ tsp salt

1 tbsp light soy sauce

2 tsp chilli bean sauce

3 tbsp tomato purée

3 tbsp finely chopped spring onions

2 tbsp finely chopped fresh coriander plus a sprig, to garnish

4 eggs, beaten

1   Place the rice in a heavy pan with 750ml/1¼ pints of water and bring to the boil. Continue boiling for 15–20 minutes or until most of the surface liquid has evaporated. By now the surface should have small indentations and look rather like a pitted crater. At this point, cover the pan with a very tight-fitting lid, reduce the heat to as low as possible and let the rice cook undisturbed for 15 minutes. Leave to go cold. The colder the rice, the better it stir fries.

2   Heat a wok or large frying pan and add the oil. When moderately hot, add the onions and stir fry for 3 minutes. Add the cold rice and stir fry for 3 minutes. Add all the remaining ingredients, except for the eggs. Stir fry for 5 minutes over a high heat. Add the beaten eggs and cook for 3 minutes or until set. Transfer to a serving plate.

Nutrition notes per serving: *530 Calories, Protein 15g, Carbohydrate 97g, Fat 12g, Saturated fat 3g, Fibre 1g, Added sugar 0g, Salt 1.12g.*

Sauces

LIGHT AND EASY SAUCE Ⓥ

Serves 2

2 tbsp hoisin sauce

1½ tbsp light soy sauce

2 tsp chilli bean sauce

1 tbsp sesame oil

225g/8oz warm, cooked dried flat rice noodles or warm, cooked dried Chinese 'fun' rice noodles, to serve

1 tbsp toasted sesame seeds, to garnish (optional)

1   Combine the hoisin sauce, soy sauce, chilli bean sauce and sesame oil and pour over the warm cooked noodles. Garnish with sesame seeds, if liked.

Nutrition notes per serving: *201 Calories, Protein 5g, Carbohydrate 22g, Fat 11g, Saturated fat 1g, Fibre 2g, Added sugar 5g, Salt 2.12g.*

FAST SPICY MEAT SAUCE

Serves 4–6

1½ tbsp groundnut (peanut) oil

2 tbsp coarsely chopped garlic

3 tbsp coarsely chopped spring onions

2 tbsp coarsely chopped fresh root ginger

450g/1lb minced pork

1 tbsp chilli bean sauce

1 tbsp dark soy sauce

2 tbsp Chinese rice wine or dry sherry

2 tbsp hoisin sauce

1 tsp salt

2 tsp sugar

1   Heat a wok or large frying pan, then add the oil. Add the garlic, spring onions and ginger and stir fry for 1 minute. Add the pork and stir fry for 2 minutes, stirring well to break up any clumps of meat.

2   Stir in the chilli bean sauce, soy sauce, rice wine or sherry, hoisin sauce, salt and sugar and cook for 5 minutes. Serve with noodles or rice.

Nutrition notes per serving when dish serves 4: *252 Calories, Protein 25g, Carbohydrate 8g, Fat 13g, Saturated fat 4g, Fibre 1g, Added sugar 5g, Salt 2.26g.*

TIP

The sauce freezes well, so you could make several batches and freeze those you do not need immediately. You can also substitute minced beef for the pork.

MIXED PEPPER SAUCE Ⓥ

TV Cooks KEN HOM COOKS NOODLES AND RICE

Serves 4

2 tbsp groundnut (peanut) oil

3 garlic cloves, crushed

175g/6oz yellow pepper, cut into 1cm/½in squares

175g/6oz red pepper, cut into 1cm/½in squares

175g/6oz green pepper, cut into 1cm/½in squares

1 tbsp yellow bean sauce

2 tbsp dark soy sauce

1 tbsp Chinese rice wine or dry sherry

2 tbsp finely chopped spring onions

150ml/¼ pint Vegetable stock (page 62)

1 tsp sugar

450g/1lb cooked dried Chinese 'fun' rice noodles, to serve

shredded spring onion, to garnish

1 Heat a wok or large frying pan and add the oil. When moderately hot, add the garlic and stir fry for 30 seconds. Add the remaining ingredients, including the cooked rice noodles and stir fry for 3 minutes or until the peppers are thoroughly cooked and the noodles are warmed through. Transfer to a warm serving dish and garnish with spring onions if desired.

Nutrition notes per serving: *179 Calories, Protein 5g, Carbohydrate 26g, Fat 7g, Saturated fat 1g, Fibre 3g, Added sugar 3g, Salt 1.36g.*

TIP

The texture of the noodles is a good contrast to that of the colourful, zesty peppers. These tender rice noodles are usually combined with beef and peppers. In this vegetarian version you could also try adding black beans.

TOMATO BEEF WITH ONIONS

Serves 4–6

450g/1lb lean beef steak, cut into thick 5mm x 5cm/¼ x 2in slices

1 tbsp light soy sauce

2 tsp Chinese rice wine or dry sherry

2 tsp cornflour

2 tbsp groundnut (peanut) oil

225g/8oz onions, cut into thick slices

450g/1lb tomatoes, quartered

3 tbsp oyster sauce

1 Place the meat slices in a bowl, add the soy sauce, rice wine or sherry and cornflour and mix well.

2 Heat a wok or large frying pan and add the oil. When hot, add the beef and stir fry for 2 minutes to brown. Using a slotted spoon, remove beef and set aside.

3 Add the onions to the wok and stir fry for 1 minute. Pour in two tablespoons of water and cook for 3 minutes. Drain the juices from the beef into the wok and cook for 2 minutes. Add the tomatoes and oyster sauce and cook until the tomatoes are just heated through. They should not be allowed to become mushy. Return the beef to the wok to heat through. Serve with noodles or rice.

Nutrition notes per serving when dish serves 4: *311 Calories, Protein 25g, Carbohydrate 13g, Fat 18g, Saturated fat 6g, Fibre 2g, Added sugar 0g, Salt 1.97g.*

Basics

BASIC VEGETABLE STOCK

Makes about 4.5 litres/8 pints

25g/1oz Chinese dried mushrooms (optional)

2 tbsp groundnut (peanut) oil

6 spring onions

6 slices fresh root ginger

8 garlic cloves, crushed

225g/8oz shallots, left whole

900g/2lb carrots, coarsely chopped

4 celery sticks, coarsely chopped

900g/2lb onions, coarsely chopped

4 leeks, white part only, coarsely chopped

1 tbsp black peppercorns

1 tbsp Sichuan peppercorns

3 tbsp light soy sauce

4 bay leaves

2 tbsp salt

1 If you are using dried mushrooms, soak in warm water for 20 minutes. Drain, squeeze out any excess liquid, then coarsely chop the caps and stalks.

2 Heat a large pan or wok over a moderate heat and add the oil. Add the spring onions, ginger, garlic and shallots and stir fry for 1 minute. Stir in the carrots, celery, onions and leeks and cook for 5 minutes. Place all the vegetables and the remaining ingredients into a very large pan. Cover with 4.5 litres/8 pints of cold water and bring to simmering point.

3 Using a large, flat spoon, skim off the foam that rises to the top; this will take about 5 minutes. Heat the stock until it is almost boiling. Reduce the heat to moderate and simmer for 2 hours.

4 Strain the stock through a large colander, then through a very fine mesh strainer. Leave to cool thoroughly. It is now ready to use or transfer to containers and freeze for future use.

STEAMED STICKY RICE

Serves 4

425ml/15fl oz glutinous or short grain rice

115g/4oz fresh or frozen peas

1 tbsp groundnut (peanut) oil

1 tbsp chopped fresh root ginger

3 tbsp finely chopped spring onions

115g/4oz mushrooms, finely sliced

2 tbsp finely chopped rinsed Sichuan preserved vegetable

3 tbsp rice wine or dry sherry

1 tbsp dark soy sauce

2 tbsp light soy sauce

1 Place the rice in a large bowl, cover with water and leave to stand for 4 hours or overnight. Drain well. Set up a steamer or put a rack inside a wok or large, deep pan. Pour in about 5cm/2in water and bring to the boil. Tip the rice into a bowl and place in the steamer or on the rack. Cover the pan tightly, reduce the heat to low and steam gently for 20 minutes. If using fresh peas, blanch in boiling water for 3 minutes, then drain well and immerse in cold water.

2 Heat a wok or large frying pan and add the oil. Add the ginger and spring onions and stir fry for 2 minutes. Add the mushrooms and preserved vegetable and cook for 5 minutes or until most of the liquid has evaporated. Add the rice wine or sherry and soy sauces and cook for 2 minutes. Stir in the steamed rice and peas.

3 Refill the steamer with hot water. Transfer the rice mixture to a bowl and steam for 30 minutes over a low heat. Serve or keep warm in the steamer, with the heat turned off, for about 30 minutes. It also reheats well.

Many of your favourite TV Cooks are also featured in a range of specially filmed half-hour BBC videos. They share the secrets of their key techniques and demonstrate some of their favourite recipes. Each video contains detailed step by step instructions on how to prepare and present creative dishes, acting as a companion to the book series.

The following are available as books and videos or as combined packs:

Ken Hom Cooks Chinese	BBCV5994
Mary Berry Cooks Cakes	BBCV6381
Mary Berry Cooks Puddings & Desserts	BBCV6193
Michael Barry Cooks Crafty Classics	BBCV6115
Nick Nairn Cooks The Main Course	BBCV6380
Rick Stein Cooks Fish	BBCV6111
Sophie Grigson Cooks Vegetables	BBCV6112
Valentina Harris Cooks Italian	BBCV6117

The following are only available as books:

Keith Floyd Cooks Barbies	0 563 38346 1
Madhur Jaffrey Cooks Curries	0 563 38794 7
Rick Stein Cooks Seafood	0 563 38453 0

INDEX

Many of your favourite TV Cooks are also featured in a range of specially filmed half-hour BBC videos. They share the secrets of their key techniques and demonstrate some of their favourite recipes. Each video contains detailed step-by-step instructions on how to prepare and present creative dishes, acting as a companion to the book series.

The following are available as books and videos or as combined packs:

Ken Hom Cooks Chinese	BBCV5994
Mary Berry Cooks Cakes	BBCV6381
Mary Berry Cooks Puddings & Desserts	BBCV6193
Michael Barry Cooks Crafty Classics	BBCV6115
Nick Nairn Cooks The Main Course	BBCV6380
Rick Stein Cooks Fish	BBCV6111
Sophie Grigson Cooks Vegetables	BBCV6112
Valentina Harris Cooks Italian	BBCV6117

The following are only available as books:

Keith Floyd Cooks Barbies	0 563 38346 1
Madhur Jaffrey Cooks Curries	0 563 38794 7
Rick Stein Cooks Seafood	0 563 38453 0

INDEX